A CHILD'S BOOK
of
FAERIES

To Joanna, Lily and Poppy — my faery
special god-daughters — T. R. B.
To my niece, Grace Isabella Newey — G. N.

Barefoot Books
124 Walcot Street
Bath
BA1 5BG

Text copyright © 2002 by Tanya Robyn Batt
Illustrations copyright © 2002 by Gail Newey

First published in Great Britain in 2002 by Barefoot Books Ltd

This book was typeset in Cochin 14pt
The illustrations were prepared in watercolour
and mixed medium on 140lb watercolour paper

Graphic design by Jester Designs, Bath
Colour separation by Grafiscan, Verona
Printed and bound in Singapore by Tien Wah Press Pte Ltd.

This book has been printed on 100% acid-free paper

ISBN 1-84148-953-0

British Cataloguing-in-Publication Data: a catalogue record
for this book is available from the British Library

3 5 7 9 8 6 4 2

A CHILD'S BOOK

of

FAERIES

collected and retold by
TANYA ROBYN BATT

illustrated by
GAIL NEWEY

Barefoot Books
Celebrating Art and Story

Contents

Contents

Introduction

When the first baby laughed for the first time, the laugh broke into a thousand pieces, and they all went skipping about and that was the beginning of faeries.

— J. M. Barrie, *Peter Pan*

For many centuries faeries have been a source of both inspiration and fascination for people from all walks of life and from many different parts of the world. While folklore and literature document faery belief in many cultures, this collection of stories and poems focuses on the beliefs and traditions characteristic of the faery folk from Britain and Ireland. *A Child's Book of Faeries* is influenced on the whole by the works of writers and artists of the Victorian era, a period in which faery lore was celebrated widely. But faery belief is much older than this, of course.

The magical realm of Fair Elf Land has frequently captured the imagination of writers, artists and musicians alike. From Shakespeare and William Blake to Arthur Rackham and J. M. Barrie, each has sought to capture his or her vision of the faery folk and the enchanting world they inhabit. These visions are varied but in their entirety express the complexity of faery belief.

There are as many different names for the faeries as there are stories about their origins. Some describe faeries as a very ancient race of people who now live beneath the ground. Others present them as ghosts of the dead, or nature spirits, while others portray faeries as fallen angels who reside neither in heaven nor in hell. In Wales they are called the Tylweth Teg, meaning the 'fair family' – for they are said to have light-coloured hair – or sometimes Bendith Ymamau, the 'mother's blessing'. In Ireland there are the Tuatha de Danann (a tall, lordly, god-like race) and the Daoine Sidhe – the 'good neighbours' or 'wee folk'. In Scotland there is the Seelie Court (the good faeries) and the Unseelie Court (the wild and wicked faery host). While sharing certain characteristics, these different groups of faeries and their associated behaviours give rise to the various stories, customs and superstitions associated with faery belief.

In *A Child's Book of Faeries* I have attempted to capture some of these different facets of the faery world through the poems, stories and pieces of folklore gathered here. In the stories, for instance, we can see faery cunning at work in 'Leprechaun Gold', their fascination with things human in 'The Faeries and the Cake Baker', their ability both to be generous and yet to inspire fear in 'The Magic Cooking Pot', and their special relationship with children in 'Only Me'. The poems selected evoke the enticing and mystical world of faery – a half-glimpsed realm of talking birds, of flight and revelry, of the miniature and the grand, presided over by the elusive, ever-watchful faery folk, whose disguise is more often than not the mantle of the night.

The stories in this collection can be regarded as both old and new. They are old in the sense that they belong to a world that existed before television, cars and computers – a time when stories told and shared provided the best 'pictures'. They are new because they open the minds of modern readers and remind us of the ever-present magic of possibility. Remember, as you turn these pages and journey through the faery realm, that what the heart believes the eye sees; and magic lies in the strength of vision – it is the kernel of knowing that to wish is to be.

— *Tanya Robyn Batt*

7

The Faery Folk

Come cuddle close in daddy's coat
Beside the fire so bright,
And hear about the faery folk
That wander in the night.
For when the stars are shining clear,
And all the world is still,
They float across the silver moon
From hill to cloudy hill.

Their caps of red, their cloaks of green,
Are hung with silver bells,
And when they're shaken with the wind
Their merry ringing swells.
And riding on the crimson moths
With black spots on their purple wings,
They guide them down the purple sky
With golden bridle rings.

They love to visit girls and boys
To see how sweet they sleep,
To stand beside their cosy cots
And at their faces peep.
For in the whole of faery land
They have no finer sight
Than little children sleeping sound
With faces rosy bright.

On tip-toe crowding round their heads,
When bright the moonlight beams,
They whisper little tender words
That fill their minds with dreams;
And when they see a sunny smile,
With lightest finger tips
They lay a hundred kisses sweet
Upon the ruddy lips.

And then the little spotted moths
Spread out their crimson wings,
And bear away the faery crowd
With shaking bridle rings.
Come, bairnies, hide in daddy's coat,
Beside the fire so bright –
Perhaps the little faery folk
Will visit you to-night.

— *Robert M. Bird*

Faery Mischief

Faeries and humans have always been suspicious of one another. Faeries, in particular, love to play practical jokes. One of the most famous mischief-makers of the faery world is Robin Goodfellow, or Puck, as later named by William Shakespeare in his play *A Midsummer Night's Dream*. Robin Goodfellow was reputed to be half faery (his father was Oberon, the faery king) and half human. He loved to play pranks on people.

One of the faeries' favourite tricks is making humans lose their way. This is called being 'pixie-led' and can happen to people even when they are travelling along a path they know well.

Faeries are shape-shifters and can disguise themselves so that they look and sound like other people or animals. The Hedley Kow was a bogie or goblin who liked to change himself into a bundle of straw. He would then be picked up by some unsuspecting person, who would find the bundle becoming heavier and heavier. Finally the puzzled person would put the bundle of straw down, whereupon it would shuffle away and give a loud laugh before disappearing altogether!

Nobody much likes having tricks played on them, and so humans have devised all kinds of ways to keep themselves safe from faery mischief. You can protect yourself from faery magic by wearing your clothes inside out, by donning odd socks or a daisy chain. Faeries do not like iron, so bells hung in doorways or a nail placed in a pocket will keep them away, as will a sprig of broom or St John's wort. Faeries don't like loud noise, nor can they abide the crowing of a rooster, which signals the dawn. They tend to be creatures of the night.

As you will see, the old farmer in this next story was rather worried about faery mischief himself.

The Magic Cooking Pot

There was once an old couple who lived together on a farm. It was a tidy little farm nestling between two hills, with a forest fringing the far fields. Now, as lovely as everything was on the farm, the most marvellous thing to be found on it was a cooking pot. But this was no ordinary cooking pot – it was a magic one.

The cooking pot belonged to the old woman. It had been her mother's and before that her grandmother's and before that her great-grandmother's. People said that her great-grandmother had been a faery and when she married into the mortal world the faeries had given her the pot as a wedding gift. The remarkable thing about this pot was that no matter how much you ate from it, it would fill itself again with food until you told it to stop. There it sat on the hearth, the old woman's prized possession, all ready for the next meal.

But the strangest thing was that every evening after supper, a wee faery man would come skipping down the hill from the forest. Without so much as a 'please' or a 'thank you' the faery would scoop up the pot and make his way back to the forest. The old woman would always call after the faery:

'A cooking pot needs meat and bones;
Be sure to bring it back with some.'

And, sure enough, every morning the pot would be returned to the hearth, in time for the old couple's breakfast. This went on year in, year out. Every day a faery would appear and collect the pot and every day the old woman would call out her chant and the pot would be returned the following morning.

One morning the old woman was called away from the farm to nurse a sick friend in a village some distance away. 'I'll be gone for a day and a night and then some,' she reminded her husband before she left. 'Be sure you remember to greet the faery politely and to say the magic words to him.'

'Of course I'll remember, old woman,' the old man gruffly replied.

When his wife had gone, the farmer made his way to the far fields to repair a fence. As he worked he peered into the forest and that made him think about the faeries. He'd heard plenty of stories about the wee folk who were said to live there, and they weren't all good. Sure enough, they might grant you a favour if you did them a good turn, but there were lots of stories about how faeries caused trouble by tricking people and bringing them bad luck. The more the old man thought about it, the more worried he grew. He didn't fancy meeting a faery – and one of them was due at the cottage that very evening! What if he said something wrong and upset the wee creature?

At the end of the day the old man quickly packed up his tools and hurried home. Reaching the cottage, he shuttered the windows and locked the door with a great iron bolt. Then he jumped into bed and pulled the covers up over his head, lying there as quiet as a mouse.

Well, it wasn't long before a faery came skipping down the hill from the forest. Finding the door of the cottage shut and barred with iron, the faery stomped his foot and flew to the top of the chimney. There he gave a whistle and the cooking pot flew from the hearth right up the chimney and straight into his hands. Then down the faery jumped, and up and over the hill he went and disappeared into the forest.

After some time, the farmer peeked out from beneath the covers. Seeing no sign of the faery, he felt a bit braver. With the faery gone, and the pot too, he set about scraping together a meal as best he could.

Late the next afternoon, the old woman arrived home. Of course, the first thing she noticed when she stepped into the cottage was that the pot was missing. Maybe the faery had already collected it, she thought, or maybe he was late in returning the pot. When the old man came in, she asked, 'Husband, did a faery come yesterday and collect the pot?'

The old man nodded his head.

'You did remember to say the words, didn't you?' said the old woman.

'I forgot,' mumbled the old man, not wanting to admit how frightened he had been.

The old woman shook her head. 'Well, that's it then,' she cried. 'We'll never see the cooking pot again.'

'I'm sure they'll bring it back,' said the old man.

'They won't,' snapped the old woman.

'Will,' argued the old man.

Will, won't, will, won't. They argued back and forth until they were hoarse. Then they both went to bed without any supper.

But the old woman was right, for the next morning there was still no sign of the pot. She waited until the afternoon, and then set out to fetch it back. Pulling on her cloak, the old woman set off uphill towards the forest. Reaching the edge of the fields, she climbed over the fence. A narrow pathway wound its way up through the leafy green woods. The old woman walked for some time. The trees grew thicker and the path narrower still. Just as the sun began to set, she came to a clearing. On the far side of the clearing rose a rock face and, tunnelled into it, the mouth of a large, dark cave.

Taking a deep breath, the old woman stepped into the gloom of the cave. After a few minutes, her eyes adjusted to the darkness and ahead of her she could see the glow of a fire which had burnt low. There, sitting on the glowing embers, was her pot. As she stepped forward to retrieve it, she noticed that, all around the fire, faery men were sleeping. They had brown ruddy faces and wore bright red caps. Lying alongside them were the faery hounds. When they were awake these dogs had eyes like saucers, long sharp teeth and could run like the wind.

The old woman didn't want to wake up the little men and she definitely didn't want to wake up the faery dogs. So she slowly reached out over their sleeping bodies and gently took hold of the pot. Then, just as she was creeping softly back towards the mouth of the cave, all of a sudden

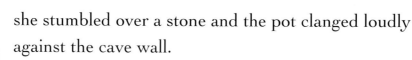

she stumbled over a stone and the pot clanged loudly against the cave wall.

Roused by the noise, the faery men jumped up. 'After her, after her!' they shrieked. 'She's stealing our pot!'

As quick as quick, the old woman dashed from the cave and back down the path, easily outrunning the faery men with their short legs. But soon she could feel the hot, damp breath of the faery hounds upon her heels. She reached into the pot and took a great handful of meat and bones and threw them over her shoulder. The dogs stopped and wolfed down the food.

Down the path the old woman ran. Once again she could hear the panting of the dogs close behind her. For a second time she threw more scraps over her shoulder, not daring to stop or look back. And again the dogs lingered to gulp down the food. The old woman's legs were aching and she was beginning to tire. In the distance she could see the lights of the cottage dimly flickering. Summoning all her strength, she raced down the hill, with the dogs in hot pursuit. They were howling now, and their paws thundered on the dewy wet grass. The old woman stopped one last time and turned the pot upside down, shaking all that was left inside it on to the ground, then stumbled on.

Now that the old woman's strength was ebbing fast, the faery hounds would easily catch her and take her back with them to Faeryland where the faeries would keep her for ever and ever. But just then the sun began to stir and creep over the horizon. The dark of the night began to lift and the rooster in the farmyard gave an almighty crow.

When the faery hounds heard the crowing of the rooster, they took fright, for they were afraid of the daylight. They ceased their pursuit of the old woman and as the first fingers of sunlight stretched across the hill they began to whine and cower. With the sun warm upon her face, the old woman felt her courage come flooding back. She turned on the dogs and called:

'You've gobbled all the meat and bones;
From this day forth you'll be getting none.'

These words ringing in their ears, the dogs turned with their tails between their legs and scurried back to the safety of the dark cave.

Joyful with relief, the old woman ran in through the front door of the cottage, to be greeted by her husband, who was very pleased to see her again. The faeries never again came to collect the pot, but it always remained full of delicious food.

And see not ye that bonny road,
Which winds about the fernie brae?
That is the road to fair Elfland,
Where you and I this night maune gae.

— *Francis James Child*

Faeryland

Fair Elfland, Elephame, Tir Nan Og – the land of the
ever young – these are some of the names for Faeryland.
Some say it lies beneath the ground in the ancient barrows
or hollow hills. Others talk of the Faery Islands, or magical
lands that lie beneath the sea or lakes, or even parallel worlds
that exist alongside our own, invisible to the human eye.

The home of the faery folk is reported to be much like
our own world, only much more beautiful. Those who have
been fortunate enough to visit and return describe magical
gardens, caves encrusted with jewels and palaces where
endless feasts take place. All things are plentiful and no one
ever grows old or ill. There are many stories told by people
who have visited Faeryland. Thomas the Rhymer and Anne
Jefferies were two people famed for their visits. Both
returned for a time to the mortal world where they became
known for their faery gifts of prophecy and healing.

Some people are kidnapped by the faeries and taken to
Faeryland, others stumble across hidden doorways in the
sides of hills. Sometimes they step inside toadstool rings, a
favourite gathering place for faeries. The white hawthorn

tree, which flowers in May, is known as the faery tree, and can mark faery pathways and entrances into Faeryland.

There are times of the year when it is easier to enter the world of Faery – May 1st, Beltane, and the eve of October 31st, Samhain. At these times the 'veil' between the human world and Faeryland is at its thinnest. The hours of magic are dawn, dusk, midday and midnight.

Faeryland is a place of great beauty and glamour. Those who visit Faeryland must be very careful, for time passes differently between the two worlds. Those who think they have spent but two days in Faeryland return to the mortal world to find that two hundred years have passed by, or alternatively two years in Faeryland can be but a blinking of an eye in our own world. Whilst in Faeryland no food or drink should be eaten, and nothing should be taken that is not freely given. Those who break these rules may find that they cannot leave Faeryland, or are never able to enter the magical realm again. Those who do return from Faeryland and please the faeries are often given gifts or rewards, as is the heroine in this next story.

The Faeries
and the Cake Baker

Once there was a woman whose name was Margaret. Now Margaret was a great cake baker. She made chocolate cakes and strawberry cakes, she made birthday cakes and wedding cakes. She made crumbling sugary shortbread and zesty lemon slices. People came from miles around to buy Margaret's cakes. They were delicious.

People from miles around weren't the only ones who loved Margaret's cakes. The faeries loved them too — whenever they got a chance to eat any! For when people ate Margaret's cakes they often forgot to leave any crumbs. When the poor faeries came for their share, not a scrap nor skerrick of cake could they find. This went on for a good long while and they began to grumble among themselves.

'It's not fair — we haven't had any of Margaret's cake for weeks and weeks!' they said. So they made a plan. They decided that they would kidnap Margaret and take her to Faeryland and there they would keep her, for ever and ever, to bake them cakes.

The very next day the faeries waited quietly, hidden under a bush at the side of the road. Every morning

Margaret would walk down the road to collect her milk from the dairy. That morning, as she rounded the corner, the faeries flew out from their hiding place and sprinkled fern root in her eyes. Now fern root contains a special kind of magic, which makes you feel sleepy. Margaret gave a great big yawn and sat down. Then she fell sound asleep, and the faeries carried her away to Faeryland.

When Margaret awoke she found a hundred pairs of little eyes watching her. Her heart began to beat quickly, but she wasn't going to let the faeries know that she was frightened. 'Oh, is this Faeryland?' she said. 'I've always wanted to come to Faeryland.'

The faeries nodded. 'Yes, this is Faeryland, Margaret, and we're going to keep you here for ever and ever to make us cakes.'

Margaret looked sadly at the faeries. They were a skinny-looking bunch. 'Doesn't anybody ever feed you cake?' she asked.

'No, nobody ever feeds us cake,' lamented the faeries.

'Well, that's a crying shame. Everyone deserves cake every now and then. I'll tell you what, I'll make you my favourite cake – a chocolate cake, with delicious thick, gooey chocolate icing.'

The faeries danced about in delight.

'Wait!' cried Margaret. 'If I'm going to bake you a cake, I'll need a few things.' And she began to list the ingredients — flour, sugar, butter, eggs, cocoa, salt and milk.

Well, when the faeries heard this long list, they stopped their dancing, for faeries don't eat the sorts of food we eat. They nibble upon nuts and berries and drink fine forest wine.

'But we don't have what you need,' they grumbled.

'Well, that's another shame,' sighed Margaret, 'for without them I can't bake you a cake … Mind you, I've an idea. My cupboards are filled with the things I need. Why don't you fly back to my home and fetch them?' Margaret's eyes twinkled as she spoke, for she had remembered that faeries cannot abide noise, and this had given her an idea.

Nodding their heads in excitement, the faeries spread their wings and flew away from Faeryland, over the fields and in through Margaret's kitchen window. There they collected the flour, sugar, butter, eggs, cocoa, salt and milk. Then back to Faeryland they flew.

'Why, thank you,' said Margaret. 'Next I'll need a bowl and a spoon for stirring.'

The faeries hunted high and low throughout Faeryland, and they brought back a bowl that was the size of an eggcup and a spoon that was no bigger than a matchstick.

Margaret shook her head. 'These are too small. Fly back to my home and fetch my big bowl and my wooden spoon.'

Well, up hopped the faeries. They spread their wings and flew over the fields back to Margaret's house. It took ten faeries to lift the bowl and five to carry the spoon.

When they returned, Margaret thanked them politely and began to mix the ingredients. First she creamed together the sugar and the butter and then she added the eggs, beating them as hard as she could. All of a sudden she stopped and sighed.

'Oh, faeries!' she said. 'Whenever I'm baking at home, I have my cat, Ginger, with me. Ginger purrs, and that purring makes me feel all peaceful. I feel nervous making a cake away from my kitchen without her. So would you be so kind as to fetch Ginger and bring her here to calm me?'

Well, the faeries wanted that chocolate cake, so they spread their wings, flew out from Faeryland, over the fields and back to Margaret's house, where they picked up Ginger, who was curled up by the fire, and carried her all the way back to Faeryland.

'Thank you kindly,' said Margaret, and she took the surprised Ginger from the faeries. She petted the cat and

Ginger began to purr loudly, but not loudly enough to disturb the faeries. Margaret began to stir the cake once more. In went the flour and cocoa, with a pinch of salt, when she stopped again.

'Oh, faeries!' she cried. 'When I bake in my own kitchen, I always have my dog, Rufus, with me. He sits on the mat, and his tail slaps on the floor and it helps me keep my rhythm with the stirring of the cake. Without him, the cake will be sure to go flat. Please would you fly back and fetch Rufus for me?'

So the faeries spread their wings, flew out of Faeryland, across the fields and back to Margaret's house. They swept up Rufus and carried him back to Faeryland.

Rufus gave Margaret a great big lick and then settled down by her feet. Once again, Margaret began to stir the cake, this time to the thump, thump, thump of Rufus's tail on the floor and the warm breathy purring of Ginger.

With all the thumping and the purring, it was a little less quiet in Faeryland, but it was still not noisy enough to bother the faeries, so they went about their business. Once again Margaret stopped her stirring.

'Ah!' she cried. 'Faeries, my baby! She will have woken from her nap, and when she finds I'm not there she will cry

and wail. And when I think of her crying and wailing, it makes me weep, and my tears will roll down into the cake mixture and make it bitter. Oh please, faeries, will you fly home and fetch my baby?'

So, once again the faeries spread their wings, flew out of Faeryland, over the fields and into Margaret's house. There they found the baby in the cot. They picked her up and carried her back to Faeryland.

When they set the baby down in Margaret's arms, she began to cry. And how that baby cried! The dog's tail thumped and the cat purred, and the noise was all too much for the little people. They put their hands over their ears and shouted crossly at Margaret.

'Make that baby stop crying!'

But Margaret just shook her head and called above the din, 'I can't stop now, I'm at a very important stage with the stirring. You might want to fetch my husband, Tom, because sometimes he can calm the baby.'

Off the faeries flew, over the fields and into Margaret's house, where they swept Tom up by the seat of his trousers. He arrived in Faeryland with a bewildered look upon his face. But hearing the baby crying and seeing Margaret so busy, he reached down to pick up the baby,

and he accidentally trod on Ginger's tail. This, of course, made Ginger yowl loudly and she leaped up in fright on to Rufus's back, digging in her claws. Rufus howled and began to bark as he tried to shake off the cat. All this commotion made the baby cry louder still.

The faeries couldn't stand it. They loved cake but they couldn't bear all that noise. They opened the doors to Faeryland and pushed Margaret, her husband Tom, the baby, Ginger the cat and Rufus the dog out into the evening air. The doors of Faeryland shut firmly behind them.

Margaret found herself and her family standing under an early night sky, in the middle of the fields, clutching her mixing bowl. She had escaped!

But Margaret had a kind heart. She felt sorry for all those faeries who never had any cake. So she finished baking the cake and smothered it with thick chocolate icing. Then she carried it back to the fields and left it at the the door of Faeryland. The faeries were so pleased when they found it that they left a purse of gold under

Margaret's pillow, just to say, 'Thank you very much.'

When mortals are at rest,
And snoring in their nest;
Unheard and unspyed,
The key holes we do glide;
Over the tables, stools and shelves
We trip it with our faery selves.

— *Anonymous*

The Faery King and Queen

O then, I see Queen Mab hath been with you.
She is the faeries' midwife, and she comes
In a shape no bigger than an agate-stone
On the forefinger of an alderman,
Drawn with a team of little atomies
Athwart men's noses as they lie asleep.

— William Shakespeare

The faery court is a magical realm, ruled over by a king or queen or sometimes both. Queen Mab is one of the names given to the faery queen. Sometimes she is described as being very small, travelling in a carriage drawn by tiny insects. Titania is another name for the faery queen, though she is larger and more elegant and regal than Mab. Both Titania and Mab have a king, who is called Oberon. He stands as tall as a small child and looks more like a dwarf. He owes his misshapen appearance to a curse that was put upon him at his christening. Other faery kings and queens include Gwyn ap Knudd (the Welsh king) and Finvarra and Oonagh (the Irish king and queen).

One of the most famous tales of the faery queen concerns the visit to Faeryland of Thomas the Rhymer, a thirteenth-century prophet and poet. One day, when out in the countryside, Thomas spied the most beautiful woman he had ever seen. She was wearing a dress of grass-green silk and rode a white horse whose mane was twined with fifty tiny silver bells. This lady, the Queen of Elfland, took Thomas to her faery kingdom, where he lived for seven years. Just before he returned to the mortal world, the queen bestowed upon him the gift of prophecy, for which he later became famous.

The Dream Faery

A little Faery comes at night,
Her eyes are blue, her hair is brown,
With silver spots upon her wings,
And from the moon she flutters down.

She has a little silver wand,
And when a good child goes to bed
She waves her hand from right to left,
And makes a circle round its head.

And then it dreams of pleasant things,
Of fountains filled with faery fish,
And trees that bear delicious fruit,
And bow their branches at a wish.

Of arbours filled with dainty scents
From lovely flowers that never fade;
Bright flies that glitter in the sun
And glow-worms shining in the shade;

And talking birds with gifted tongues
For singing songs and telling tales,
And pretty dwarfs to show the way
Through faery hills and faery dales.

— *Thomas Hood*

Faeries and Children

Faeries seem to have a particularly weak spot for human children. Where children are concerned, faeries can be especially generous and especially mischievous. Some of the best-known stories about faeries tell of them stealing children from their human parents. Human babies are especially vulnerable if they have not been given a name or baptised. More often than not, the human baby is replaced with a faery changeling – a bad-tempered, sickly-looking child, who has a huge appetite. The most common way to flush out a changeling is to set about 'brewing in eggshells' – putting water and grain into empty eggshells and placing them in front of the fire. If the baby says, 'I have seen the first acorn before the oak, but I never saw brewing done in eggshells before,' then you can be sure that it is a changeling. Human babies are stolen because they are usually much stronger and healthier than faery babies.

Human children often find it easier to see faery folk than adults do. Whether this is because adults are simply unable to see them through lack of belief, or that faeries are more attracted by children's beauty and playfulness, it is

difficult to say. When they lose their milk teeth, children are visited by the tooth faeries, and the knots that parents find so tricky to tease out of their children's hair of a morning are known as 'faery-locks', made by the faeries who play with children's hair while they are sleeping.

But it is not just human children who are privy to Faeryland. One of the most famous encounters between faeries and people is that of the 'green children'. These two faery children, a boy and a girl, were found in the twelfth century in Suffolk. Their skin was green and at first they ate only green beans. The boy became ill and died soon afterwards, but the girl lived on quite happily and in good health. As she began to eat other sorts of food, she gradually lost her green colouring. She explained how she had come from a country where everyone was green and how one day she and the boy had been exploring a cavern together when they suddenly found themselves in the human world.

Many children wish that they could meet a faery. I wonder if they still would after reading this next story.

Only Me

Beth did not like going to bed. Every night it was the same. Her mother would ask her nicely to put on her nightdress, to have a drink of water and to say her prayers. But Beth would pretend not to hear. She would sit and draw pictures in the ashes on the warm hearthstone. She would build small huts from the kindling and compose funny little songs in her head.

Beth's mother would say again, 'Come on now, Beth, it's time for your sleep.'

Then Beth would beg to stay up for just a minute longer, or ask her mother some tricky question, such as 'What makes the fire crackle?' or 'Why can't you feel the smoke from the flames?'

Then Beth's mother would frown, and her voice would become stiff and sharp: 'Elizabeth Jane, you get yourself up from the floor and put that body of yours into bed, before I count to five … one, two, three, four, four and a half, four and three-quarters … five!'

But still Beth would linger by the fire. Her mother would plead and shout and threaten to punish the little girl, but no matter what she did, Beth would not go to bed.

Well, it was on one such evening that this tale begins. It was winter and the days were short and grey and the nights long and black. The wind howled outside, wisps of its breath burrowed through the thatch and whistled through the rafters. Beth and her mother had finished their supper, and as Beth's mother collected up the bowls she muttered, ''Tis a wild night tonight. The safest place to be, I'd say, would be in bed.' She turned to Beth: 'Now come on, girl – get yourself ready.'

But Beth liked the whining of the wind, and the flames of the fire seemed brighter and more lively than usual. She watched the tongues of orange and red dance and lick about the blackened wood. 'Ma, why do you think it is that the wind cries like that?' she asked.

''Tis the sound of the exasperated mothers who cannot get their children to bed,' answered Beth's mother rather crossly. 'Now to bed please, Beth.'

Beth pulled her apron down tight over her knees, and listened harder to the wailing of the wind.

'It makes you feel all tingly-like, don't you think, Ma?'

'I'll give you tingly,' growled her mother. 'You best listen to me, Elizabeth Jane. It's not a good night to be sitting by the fire. The wind calls all sorts out. Why, if you keep sitting there, I wouldn't be surprised to find you gone in the morning.' Beth's mother stood over her with her hands resting on her hips.

'Gone? Why, where would I go?' asked Beth, more interested in her mother's story than bothered by the frown on her face.

'The faeries might come and snatch you away,' replied her mother, 'and maybe I'd be lucky and they'd give you back with new ears – ones that listen. Now go to bed!'

Beth liked the idea of faeries. 'Do you really think so, Ma? I think I would like to meet a faery. Can I wait a wee bit longer to see if one comes?'

Beth's mother threw her arms up in despair. 'I'll not waste my breath any more. Nor my own rest. I'm going to bed.' And with that she grumpily climbed the ladder up into the loft and left Beth sitting by the fire.

Beth picked up a stick and poked it at the glowing embers, causing a spray of sparks to sail up the chimney. It would be nice to have a faery friend, she thought to herself. And she'd not been sitting there for long when the wind gave a particularly loud howl, which caused the windows to rattle and the door to creak. There came a thump upon the roof and a fluttering sound from the chimney, and then, all of a sudden, a tiny wee girl dropped from the chimney and landed alongside Beth.

She didn't come any higher than Beth's knee; her hair was fine and long like silvery-spun spider webs, her eyes as green as the grass and her cheeks were round and apple-red.

Beth was both surprised and pleased. 'Hello,' she said. 'Have you come to play with me?'

The faery's eyes twinkled with mischief and she nodded her silvery head.

'What's your name?' asked Beth.

'I've many names,' replied the faery child, hopping from one foot to the other.

'How many?' asked Beth. She was very curious to know, having only the two herself.

'Well, I've one for the day and one for the night. And one each for my mother and my father. Then there's the name that the wind calls and the one you can hear in the river –' the faery child suddenly stopped her sing-song list. Her green eyes fixed upon Beth: 'Why, what are you called?'

Beth felt rather ashamed that she had only the two names – Elizabeth and Jane – neither of which sounded as grand as ones spoken by the river or the wind. She didn't know what to say and so she muttered, 'I'm only me.'

'Only Me! That's a funny name,' laughed the faery. 'Well, what shall we play, Only Me?'

Beth showed the faery how to draw pictures in the ash. Together they drew animals, trees, houses and people. They were the best pictures that Beth had ever drawn, for when the faery child blew upon them, they came to life. The animals lumbered and prowled about the hearth and the trees swayed in the wind. From the houses poured tiny people, who gaily played and talked with one another.

They built small huts from the kindling, and when the faery tapped the twigs with her finger, they began to sprout first buds, then blossom and finally shiny green leaves. Then they plucked the leaves from the sticks and lined them up upon the hearthstone, and the faery caused each leaf to whistle, so together the leaves played a funny little tune. Beth and the faery held hands and danced.

Soon they grew tired of this game and so they sat and watched the fire. The faery made the flames turn into small people, who danced and dipped in fine dresses of red, orange and yellow satins and silks.

As the night wore on, the fire began to die down. Beth picked up a stick and gave the embers a poke to stir them into flame. As she prodded one of the logs, it crackled and all of a sudden a red-hot spark jumped from the fire and landed upon the faery child's foot.

The faery child gave such a shriek that Beth felt sure her mother would wake. Beth tried to calm the faery and to put water on her wee foot, but she would not stand still. She hopped about the hearth, her squealing growing louder and louder so that finally Beth was forced to clamp her hands over her ears. It sounded as if all the wind in the world was whistling through one tiny keyhole.

All of a sudden there was another thump upon the roof, and again a fluttering sound came from the chimney. This time Beth did not wait to see what appeared. She dashed up the ladder into the loft and hid under the blankets of her bed. From under the blankets she heard a voice boom down the chimney.

'What is the matter, my child?'

'Ah, Mother,' sobbed the little faery child, ''tis my foot. It's burnt.'

'And who did this to you?' came the voice from the chimney, this time angrily. 'Tell me who and they will be punished.'

'Only Me did it. Only Me burnt my foot,' the faery

child cried back, squealing and squealing worse than ever!

'Then why are you making such a fuss, if you did it yourself?' boomed the voice.

Beth thought the voice sounded much closer now. She peeked from beneath her blankets, just in time to see the long, white arm of the faery mother stretch down through the chimney and pluck up the faery child. In a blink the tiny girl had disappeared.

Beth lay in her bed hardly daring to breathe. She waited a long time, listening, just in case the faery child or her mother returned, but all she could hear was the howling of the wind outside.

Well, the next night Beth's mother was hugely surprised. Before she'd even asked, Beth had pulled on her nightdress, said her prayers and was tucked under her blankets in the loft. And it was the same the next night and every night after that. Beth would now happily agree with her mother that bed was the safest place to be after dark, for she was in no hurry to meet the faery child again or the faery's mother with her great booming voice.

'Well, goodness me,' exclaimed Beth's mother happily, 'perhaps the faeries did bring you new ears after all!'

Faeries, black, grey, green and white,
You moonshine revellers, and shades of night.

— *William Shakespeare*

Faeries of All Kinds

The faery realms are comprised of all manner of faery folk – elves, pixies, brownies, dwarfs, trows, phoukas, boggarts and hobgoblins, just to name a few. All have their own characteristics. Some faeries like to live with humans, such as the Buttery Spirit, who feeds on poor-quality food sold in taverns by dishonest landlords, or brownies, who complete the unfinished chores about the house. Some faeries, such as elves, are often sighted in groups and referred to as 'trooping faeries'. Others, such as leprechauns, prefer their own company and are referred to as 'solitary faeries'.

The Irish leprechaun is a shoemaker. He is a small man, clothed in green, with a leather apron and a red hat. Leprechauns are also famed for their treasure, which is called 'leprechaun gold'. Now faery treasure can be a tricky thing. Faery gold, in particular, has a nasty habit of turning into leaves and nuts and the like, especially if the treasure is stolen. To find leprechaun gold, one first has to catch a leprechaun and make him promise to tell you where the gold is hidden. But knowing and finding are two different things, as you will discover in this next story.

elf

brownie

phouka

pixies

boggart

dwarf

leprechaun

Leprechaun Gold

One warm summer evening Paddy was making his way home from his day's work when all of a sudden he heard a tap-tap-tapping sound coming from the hedge at the side of the road. Paddy stopped and listened. Well, it wasn't a bird, nor did it sound like any other creature that might live in the hedgerow. Paddy walked to the edge of the road and quietly pushed the thick leafy tangle to one side and peered through the gap he had made. And what did he see but a little man sitting in the field, and alongside him was a small pile of tiny shoes, each shoe no bigger than Paddy's thumb. There were red shoes, and green shoes, and ones with large fancy buckles. The little man sat upon a little wooden stool, tapping away at one of those tiny shoes. He was dressed in green as bright and fresh as the spring grass, with a leathery apron and a bright red cap.

Paddy couldn't believe his eyes or his luck. It was a leprechaun! He hardly dared blink, for he knew if he took his eyes off that wee man the leprechaun would disappear and, with him, Paddy's chances of ever finding the faery's crock of gold.

Quietly Paddy stepped backwards and crept around the side of the hedge, over the stile and into the field. Slowly and stealthily he moved through the long grass until he was standing right behind the little man. Then he stretched out his long, strong arm and snatched the leprechaun off his wee stool and held him by the scruff of his shirt.

The little man kicked and hollered: 'Put me down, you great lug.'

'I'll put you down quick enough, once you've told me what I want to know,' said Paddy with a broad grin.

'You've no right to be interfering with a man's work,' the leprechaun shouted. 'Can't you see I'm busy?'

'Well, I won't be keeping you long from your work,' replied Paddy. 'Just show me where you've hidden your gold, and I'll let you go.'

'Gold,' spluttered the little man, 'do you see any gold?'

'Well, of course not,' snorted Paddy. 'You wouldn't just leave it lying about, would you? Now tell me where you've hidden it.'

'I haven't got any gold, you great thug. Now put me down!' shouted the leprechaun as he dangled in mid-air.

'What do you take me for?' growled Paddy. 'A fool? I

know you've got gold and I won't let you go until you tell me where it is.' Paddy gave the little man a shake and had such a fierce look in his eyes that the leprechaun let out a squeal.

'All right, I'll tell you,' he said, 'but you'll have to put me down so I can show you where it is.'

'You're a cunning little fellow,' laughed Paddy. 'If I put you down, you'll run away. So I tell you what, I'll hold on to this until I'm sure you'll keep your promise.' And with that Paddy snatched the red cap off the leprechaun's head and lowered the little man to the ground.

So the two of them set off, the leprechaun out in front and Paddy following behind, with the little man's red cap tucked into his shirt pocket. Across the field, and then across another, through a small thicket of trees, up and down ditches, over a boggy marsh and across a small stream they went. Paddy's boots were wet and his legs were beginning to ache with tiredness and his stomach to grumble with hunger. At last they came to a field covered with thistles.

'There,' the leprechaun pointed to a large thistle plant that stood among hundreds of others. 'If you dig under that one, you'll be finding the gold that you want.'

Paddy grinned from ear to ear. Gold! He was going to

be a rich man. Then he remembered he hadn't got a spade with him to dig up the treasure. For a minute there Paddy began to panic – what good was gold if it was stuck in the ground? Suddenly he had an idea. He bent over and, unfastening his shoe, he peeled a wet, smelly sock off his foot, hobbled over and tied it to the thistle plant the leprechaun had pointed out.

'Will you give me back my cap now?' asked the little man, glaring up at Paddy.

'Surely,' smiled Paddy, 'so long as you promise not to touch that sock while I go and fetch a spade.'

'Now why would I want to be touching your smelly old sock? My hat, please.' The leprechaun stretched out his hand towards Paddy.

Paddy took the cap from his top pocket and tossed it down to the little man. The leprechaun caught it and pulled it tightly back on to his head. 'Enjoy your gold,' he laughed gleefully, and then in a wink and a blink, he was gone.

Paddy hurried home and fetched a spade. Then back across the fields he ran, through the trees, up and over the ditches, across the marshland. With a leap he cleared the stream. As he ran, he thought of all the things he would do with the faery gold. Why, he'd buy himself some smart new

clothes, and a good horse and perhaps a carriage. He'd eat the finest food there was and throw a party for all his friends and family – a great party that would go on for seven days and seven nights – and he'd hire the finest fiddlers, and there'd be singing and dancing. And he'd dance with his sweetheart and buy her a fine golden ring and ask her to marry him. Paddy had spent that gold ten times over by the time he reached the thistle field.

The sun was just beginning to set and the field itself was doused in a rich golden glow. He looked out across that field and gave a cry of dismay. Every thistle bush as far as his eye could see was tied with a sock. And every single sock was the same as his very own. Poor Paddy! He would have been there for days digging all those thistles up. So heaving the spade back upon his shoulder, Paddy trudged home, without even so much as a copper penny.

Paddy never saw that leprechaun again, though sometimes, when he was out in the fields working, he felt sure he could hear a mischievous chuckle coming from the hedge. And whenever he pulled on his socks of a morning, Paddy would remember just how close he had come to finding the leprechaun's gold.

The Faeries

Up the airy mountain,
Down the rushy glen,
We daren't go a-hunting,
For fear of little men;
Wee folk, good folk,
Trooping all together;
Green jacket, red cap,
And white owl's feather!

Down along the rocky shore
Some make their home,
They live on crispy pancakes
Of yellow tide-foam;
Some in the reeds
Of the black mountain lake,
With frogs for their watch-dogs,
All night awake.

High on the hill-top
The old King sits;
He is now so old and grey,
He's nigh lost his wits.
With a bridge of white mist
Columbkill he crosses
On his stately journeys
From Slieveleague to Rosses;
Or going up with music
On cold, starry nights,
To sup with the Queen
Of the gay Northern Lights.

By the craggy hill-side
Through the mosses bare,
They have planted thorn-trees
For pleasure here and there.
Is any man so daring
As dig them up in spite,
He shall find their sharpest thorns
In his bed at night.

Up the airy mountain,
Down the rushy glen,
We daren't go a-hunting,
For fear of little men;
Wee folk, good folk,
Trooping all together;
Green jacket, red cap,
And white owl's feather!

— *William Allingham*

Sources

Stories

The Magic Cooking Pot

This is one of the first stories I ever told. I have always liked it because the faeries in it are bolder and fiercer than usual. It is a Scottish tale, probably one originally told by a storyteller to listeners gathered around a fire on which a pot very like the one in the story would have sat. I can't recall where I first came across this story, but you can find a version of it in *The Well at the World's End: Folktales of Scotland* by N. and M. Montgomerie (Bodley Head, London, 1975).

The Faeries and the Cake Baker

This is another Scottish tale – from the Highlands. I've told it for many years and in the course of its frequent retellings added details of my own. I first came across the story in *Heather and Broom* by Leclaire G. Algers (Holt, Rinehart and Winston, New York, 1960), under the title of 'The Woman who Flummoxed the Faeries'. 'Flummoxed' is a marvellous word to use here. It means to confuse or befuddle – something that faeries are very good at doing. (Even if they are the ones being 'flummoxed' in this story!)

Only Me

'Only Me' is a wonderful story, and one that easily demonstrates the way stories form part of a great big ancient family. The faery's misunderstanding of the child's name in the tale is just like that of the Cyclops when Odysseus tricks him in order to escape from his cave – a story that is one of the many great tales from ancient Greece. There are lots of different versions of the tale retold here. My retelling developed as a result of my experiences of trying to put my sister and five younger brothers to bed, but another version of the story can be found in *English Fairy Tales* by Joseph Jacobs (Frederick Muller, London, 1942).

Leprechaun Gold

This is an old Irish tale – and a good one! I've both read several versions and heard it told in various forms. F. M. Pilkington in his version of the tale, in *Shamrock and Spear: Tales and Legends from Ireland* (Bodley Head, London, 1966), refers also to the leprechaun drinking beer – another famous Irish cultural icon.

Poems

Most of the poems that I have chosen for this collection were written in the nineteenth century. These are: Robert M. Bird, 'The Faery Folk', Francis James Child, 'And see not ye that bonny road', from *The English and Scottish Popular Ballads* (5 vols, 1882–98); 'When mortals are at rest', lines from 'The Faery Queen', author unknown (date unknown, probably seventeenth century); Thomas Hood, 'The Dream Faery', William Allingham, 'The Faeries', from *Poems* (1850).

The lines I used from the plays of William Shakespeare are: 'O then, I see Queen Mab hath been with you', from *Romeo and Juliet*, Act 1, Scene 4, lines 53–8; and 'Faeries, black, grey, green and white', from *The Merry Wives of Windsor*, Act 5, Scene 5, lines 43–4.

Faery Folklore

Faery folklore is a fascinating area. For some, faery belief is still very strong, but in many parts of the world it has nearly faded from consciousness. We have folklorists to thank for the stories and lore preserved today in books. The faery folklore that is shared in this collection comes from many different sources, both written and oral. I am particularly grateful to Katharine Briggs, whose work I have always found so inspiring and thorough.

Bibliography

Briggs, Katharine, *Abbey, Lubbers, Banshees and Boggarts: A Who's Who of Fairies* (Kestrel Books, Middlesex, 1979).

— *A Dictionary of Fairies, Hobgoblins, Brownies, Bogies and Other Supernatural Creatures* (Penguin Books, Harmondsworth, 1976).

Edgar, M. G. (ed.), *A Treasury of Verse for Little Children* (Harrap, London, 1985).

Froud, Brian, and Lee, Alan, *Faeries*, ed. David Larkin (Books for Pleasure, London, 1978).

Rose, Carol, *Spirits, Fairies, Gnomes and Goblins: An Encyclopedia of the Little People* (ABC – CLIO, Santa Barbara, 1996).

Stiles, Eugene, *A Small Book of Faeries* (Pomegranate Artbooks, San Francisco, 1995).

Sullivan, Karen (ed.), *The Little Book of Faeries* (Brockhampton Press, London, 1996).

Barefoot Books
Celebrating Art and Story

At Barefoot Books, we celebrate art and story with books that open
the hearts and minds of children from all walks of life, inspiring them
to read deeper, search further, and explore their own creative gifts.
Taking our inspiration from many different cultures, we focus on
themes that encourage independence of spirit, enthusiasm for
learning, and acceptance of other traditions. Thoughtfully prepared
by writers, artists and storytellers from all over the world, our
products combine the best of the present with the best of the past to
educate our children as the caretakers of tomorrow.

www.barefootbooks.com